Thar[illegible] Mofst

Tinder: A Comprehensive Guide To Success

‘This book changed my life’

First Reader

Are you currently nursing a sprained thumb from right-swiping through Tinder so hard your broadband can’t keep up, and yet, after all of that, you don’t have a date?

It’s probably time to quit working harder and to start working smarter.

Contents

Disclaimer

This guide to Tinder is presented solely for educational and entertainment purposes. The author is simply offering their own personal views and advice which has been attained through carrying out substantial amounts of research and technique-testing when using the Tinder dating app. Whilst best efforts have been used in preparing this book, the author and publisher make no representations or warranties of any kind and assume no liabilities of any kind with respect to the accuracy or completeness of the contents and specifically disclaim any implied warranties of merchantability or fitness of use for a particular purpose. Neither the author nor the publisher shall be held liable or responsible to any person or entity with respect to any loss or incidental or consequential damages caused, or alleged to have been caused, directly or indirectly, by the information contained herein. No warranty may be created or extended by sales representatives or written sales materials. Every match or 'situation' on Tinder is different and the advice and strategies contained herein may not be suitable for your situation. The author is not claiming to be a competent professional in this field and any suggested strategies or advice are not absolutely guaranteed to succeed. In this guide, any mentioned character or entity's likeness to actual persons, either living or dead, is strictly coincidental.

Additionally, my confidants and I would like to make it very clear that we have only been using Tinder in order to write this guide. Despite organising the dates, we do not actually go on any. If we were to go on such serial-dating sprees this would no doubt be disrespectful to the people we have matched with and that's the last thing we want as this whole guide's purpose is strictly in the name of education.

Preface

All too often, when discussing the art of Tinder with my associates who use the dating app, I receive a downhearted response: 'I never seem to have any luck on there'. Repeatedly hearing such sorrowful words is enough to bring a tear to anyone's eye, and has driven us to produce this comprehensive guide to gaining success in the obscure world that is, Tinder. With the help of a few of my closest confidants (and fellow Tinder users), we aimed to produce a guide through every step of the Tinder process. This begins with that warm fuzzy feeling you get when you receive that 'You've got a new match' notification, all the way through to the ultimate achievement, your first Tinder date.

Please do remember that the techniques and strategies advocated in this book are not an absolute guarantee to achieving success on Tinder. They are techniques which have been developed, tried and tested by my confidants and I, which have no doubt played an enormous part in successfully organising a Tinder date.

Additionally, the strategies advocated in the guide will only assist in getting you to the stage where hopefully, your Tinder match agrees to go on a date with you. After this point, the success on the date will ultimately depend on yourself and your match. After all, as the great Sir Winston Churchill once said, 'it takes two to tango', and such words are scarcely more applicable than in the world of Tinder.

While this book may seem very male-orientated, it is important to remember that our research has indicated that generally on Tinder, the male will be the first to send the message. However, such techniques can be used by either a male or female user. It ultimately boils down to who is sending the first message, for which our techniques and strategies can then be utilised.

Additionally, thanks to most dating apps having a similar format, all techniques advocated in this book can be adopted across the board. This include Hinge, Bumble and if you're really rogue, Plenty of Fish, which is more notorious for its kidnapping stories that match-making.

Can I use these techniques to 'chirps' people?

I know what you're thinking. What on God's green pastures is chirpsing? It's an all-encompassing term and it cannot be boiled down to any one situation. 'Chirpsing', or the 'chirpsing stage' can broadly be described as all of the stages leading up to a first date, but this will predominantly involve texting prior to the date.

The term is also simply but effectively defined by the Urban Dictionary below.

'To chirps is to chat up, woo, or court another person'.

Example

Boy 1: Woah mate, that girl's a 10!
Boy 2: Chirps her then!

To answer your question, yes. Many of these tips and techniques apply to the 'chirpsing stage' but I trust that the reader will be able to work out which tips may apply and when.

Chapter 1: Setting up your profile and bio and the importance of getting 'verified'

Once you download Tinder and get your account set up, you will need to create your profile. This predominantly involves selecting your photos and writing a bio. I will first explain my top tips on photo selection followed by key advice on writing a good bio.

Photo Selection

I have compiled a list of the top tips provided from Tinder itself for further analysis against my own experiences. Prior to this I would suggest that the ideal number of photos is between 3 and 5. There is no golden number but any less than 3 could make you look like you're hiding something, and the last thing you want to be doing is inadvertently catfishing someone.

Tip One: Show your face

This may appear to be blindingly obvious but you would be surprised by the amount of profiles that fall victim to such a mindless error. Covering your face can have the effect of making you seem unconfident, and unless you've been living under a rock since your first romantic interaction, you'll be aware that confidence is one of the most attractive traits in a person.

Tip Two: Do not post a picture with your best friend of the opposite sex

Ignore this at your own risk. Go for it, what have you got to lose? Fast forward two weeks.

You've been left swiped so many times you've got whiplash.

Now I have your attention? I thought so. I am a strong advocate of this tip. I'm afraid for obvious reasons I cannot speak from a female's point of view on the matter.

However, I am personally less inclined to swipe right on a girl who has a guy in her picture. After all, the last thing you want is your first photo to inspire questions such as 'is this your sibling or your ex?'.

Tip Three: Lose the gym selfie or 'rig pic'

You're not wrong to jump to the assumption that a picture of your Zeus-like torso should be shown off in order to improve my match-count. I know why you may be thinking this. First and foremost, you will think back to the great words of Aristotle: 'if you've got it, flaunt it' (384 BC). However, a lot has changed since those days and the use of a gym selfie in your profile may just push you to the wrong side of that golden balance between self-doubt and arrogance. This is evidenced by a survey carried out by Planet Fitness (shape.com) who surveyed 2000 females in total, and 69% of the women who participated found the 'dadbod' sexy and 47% of women said that the dadbod is 'the new six-pack'. While you may be devastated to hear of such changes in social norms, I think the importance of adapting to such changes is embodied effectively in the quote below.

'If you want to fly, you have to give up what weighs you down' (Roy T. Bennet).

My closest confidant, who shall remain nameless, undertook some vital research on the matter and I hate to say it but the proof is in the pudding. Tinder has a 'boost' feature, which allows your profile to be seen by 10x as many users for 30 minutes. For his first boost, he used his normal 5 pictures with not a gym selfie in sight. For his second he added a fairly impressive 'gym selfie' to his profile. Despite not even using the topless picture as his first picture on display, he received 34% less matches in his second boost. Despite his initial euphoria derived from his 12 new matches, he was absolutely shocked after the second boost and endured some serious self-loathing. That is until he wisely remembered that he undertook such a bold move for strictly research-based purposes.

The Bio

You'll be glad to hear that this part requires far less thought and ultimately shouldn't hamper your efforts. However, it is the perfect chance to come across as funny or witty. You have various options. Firstly, you could go rogue and have no bio. I personally don't know the effect of doing this but it can't do much harm as it's a fairly popular choice on Tinder. Secondly, you could keep it simple with stating the area where you live or some fact which you deem absolutely essential for your future match to know. This can be helpful to avoid wasting time on conversations only to eventually find out that your 21-year-old match who is still at university isn't keen on meeting you and your two young-children. Who would've thought?

I personally have the bio of 'often described as the full package' but it's difficult to tell whether this enhances or diminishes my chances of securing that hallowed match. Additionally, I am unsure of whether it strikes that fine balance between being confident but not being arrogant. Your choice of bio will ultimately depend on you and what sort of person you want to attract. If you're looking for someone to enjoy a Chicken Caeser salad and a smoothie with, why not say that you enjoy historical literature and long walks in the park? If you're looking for someone even remotely amusing, I would suggest thinking of something slightly more compelling.

Verification

Getting your profile verified by Tinder is somewhat of an unknown gem. This is easily done by clicking on the grey tick next to your name and Tinder will then ask you to take two selfies in obscure poses. Tinder then compares the pictures and confirms you are who you say you are. This has a positive effect on your profile for two main reasons.

Firstly, this avoids any risk of a potential match thinking you look dodgy and may not be who you really are. Hopefully if you're reading this you are not one of these strange men on Tinder, but if you are, I'm not sure this guide is for you.

Secondly, it is no secret that having a blue tick by your name on Instagram is an ultimate power move, and despite having completely different meanings, having the blue tick on your Tinder has a similar effect. It makes you come across as official and legitimate. It's hard to explain this and you'll only really grasp the effect it has once you stumble across a blue-tick profile yourself. As one of my confidants explained, after getting his profile verified, and while swiping the same amount of people per day, his match rate picked up by 28%. It just goes to show that the finer details really do count.

Chapter 2: Mindset Prior To Messaging

Overlook this chapter at your peril; being in the correct mindset is instrumental to a successful DM slide-in. If you're in the wrong state of mind, prepare to enter a merciless tailspin of sudden message-regret, pathetic attempts to walk back on the mortally wounded animal that your chat has become, and for your inevitable rejection.

Being confident and self-assured is the most important thing and bonus points for being cheeky, charming and, best of all, suave. How you bring out these things in yourself is up to you. Adorn a suede dinner jacket with a maroon cummerbund, while holding a tall-stemmed frosted martini glass if necessary.

A cheeky and self-confident approach is one thing but go in too cocky and you'll be shut down like a COVID-ridden leisure centre. First impressions are everything and if you approach your match like a complete cretin, their first impression will most likely be that you are in fact a complete cretin.

On the flipside, if you approach your match with your tail between your legs, you're also pissing in the wind. Your match will sense that you don't believe that you have a chance with them, and they will probably agree. The caveat is that self-deprecation, when done right, can be both charming and humorous. Find the balance. Balance is key.

Chapter 3: Diving into the DMs (Sending the first message)

The fantastic thing about Tinder is once you've passed the 'match stage', the world really is your oyster. At this point, nothing else matters but your chat, and rightly so. Everything will be weighing on that essential first message so deciding what content to use is absolutely critical.

In this chapter I am going to explain the tried and tested chat up lines used by my confidants and I alongside their percentage success rate in achieving a reply (for every 50 messages sent to matches). Ultimately, receiving a reply is the beacon of success when it comes to sending the first message. One thing should be made absolutely clear: do not use a random chat-up line off the internet. These are used all the time and they lack originality, purely on this basis. All it takes is for 'the one' to google search 'best chat up lines' and your once seemingly witty chat up line lands you in 'the one's' cemetery of removed matches.

First Message Option 1

'You're hotter than the bottom of my laptop and I've had that for 8 years'

This line really is the undefeated champion of chat-up lines. It contains the perfect balance of wit and flattery and you can virtually guarantee a response. The stats below really do speak for themselves.

This line received a reply from our matches 47/50 times. That's a 94% success rate; the stuff of dreams. I will now analyse various responses and give the reader an opportunity to understand what sort of response they may get when sending out such top-draw content; you're welcome in advance.

Figure 1

YOU MATCHED 05/07/2020.
Hola x
You're hotter that the bottom of my laptop
And I've had that for 8 years x
Sent
Yesterday 23:16
Hola You've drawn me in already! Laptops can get pretty hot so I take that as a compliment

As you can see from the reply, this line epitomises the perfect chirps. The reply received in Figure 1 speaks for itself and consequently there is in no need for further analysis. However, it must be said that you cannot expect a response as keen as this every time but we can well-nigh guarantee a response of sorts if you have already matched with them.

This line's greatest asset is being completely original and it usually produces more than just an 'aha' response. With this line, play close attention to the use of 'Hola'. While European vibes may spring to mind, the use of Hola generally receives more replies than a 'hi or hello' and is evidently far less vanilla than the latter. Additionally, we found that splitting this message into three lines is effective as the 'I've had it for 8 years' itself as a message is very aloof so your match is bound to at least go onto the message to read it.

Figure 2

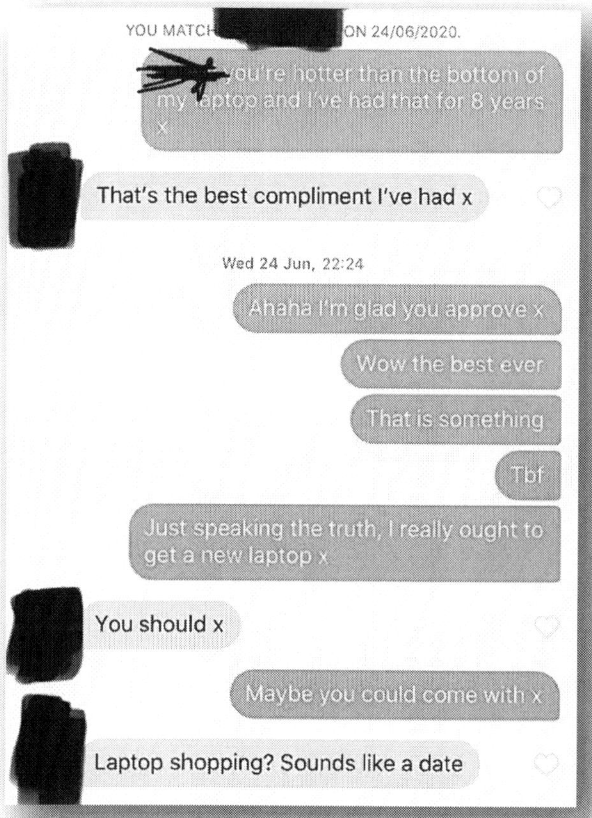

YOU MATCH ON 24/06/2020.
you're hotter than the bottom of my laptop and I've had that for 8 years x
That's the best compliment I've had x
Wed 24 Jun, 22:24
Ahaha I'm glad you approve x
Wow the best ever
That is something
Tbf
Just speaking the truth, I really ought to get a new laptop x
You should x
Maybe you could come with x
Laptop shopping? Sounds like a date

Lost for words? I know you are. Imagine how my confidant felt when serving up this line, only to have a confirmed date in 21 minutes from start to finish. Additionally, pay close attention to the follow up lines which can absolutely be applied after using this line. These three messages can be copied and your match's responses are unlikely to throw a spanner in the works. We are literally spoon feeding you Tinder success, but we wouldn't have it any other way. After all, this is a *comprehensive* guide to success.

Use of the 'x'; the secret weapon

This applies across the board in all forms of the chirps, whether it be on Tinder or another platform. The use of an 'x', alternatively known as the text form of a kiss, is always underestimated. People don't realise that the use of an 'x' alongside, or at the end of, a pure-flames line like that discussed after Figure 1, is incredibly effective. It can turn a seemingly monotone message into one that has flirty connotations and this is exactly the sort of subtle-impact chirpsing we're looking for. After all, you don't need to be a rocket scientist to know that laying it on thick will usually leave you empty-handed. (see below).

‘Treat them mean, keep them keen’ (Martin Luther King, Jr. 1935).

Figure 3

YOU MATCHED WIT N 25/06/2020.
Hey x
FYI
You're hotter that the bottom of my laptop and I've had that for 8 years x
Thu 25 Jun, 10:30
Morning,
Well that was bloody brill ain't
*brilliant x

The laptop line is a simple no-brainer. Figure 3 just emphasises that success is bound to be on the cards. Even if this line is the only valuable advice you gain from this guide, you can count your lucky stars you stumbled across the goldmine that is ‘the laptop line’.

See below for early feedback of this line used by one of my newly-recruited researchers who describes it as ‘actually lethal’.

<u>Figure 4: Their words not mine</u>

Im enjoying the tinder book btw
Laptop line is acc lethal too

MOI

Thank you I’m glad

Figure 5: Dead in the water

YOU MATCHED WIT ON 22/06/2020.
Hola x
You're hotter than the bottom of my laptop
And I've had that for 8 years
Mon 22 Jun, 10:33
Hey ounds like you should get a new laptop - wouldn't want it overheating x
Maybe I could borrow yours x
Mon 22 Jun, 11:23
Hmm you'd be v lucky - not a fan of sharing x

Clearly the recipient of this belter of a line is somewhat less impressed and—unless she is moonlighting as a sales assistant at PC World—it is likely that her matter-of-fact "get a new laptop" advice stems from a point of fundamental indifference towards the sender. If she wasn't unimpressed before, the complete lack of wit in their reply will have certainly sealed the deal. In writing "maybe I could borrow yours x", the sender is clearly wheezing for a clever reply with flirtatious insinuation, but the only thing that they are managing to insinuate is that they are looking to do a runner with her personal electronics.

This is testament to the strength of the opening line but also that the line will only get you so far. Clearly this is a fish who's reluctant to bite, but the laptop line was just too intriguing and amusing not to reply to. The sender simply has to work on their follow-up.

First Message Option 2

You: 'I'm trying to sort out my bills but I'm struggling with the math. What's 23-13?'

Your match (hopefully): 10?

You: 'What? No, it's (enter match's name) x'

This line is also an ideal option to use for the first message, and it comes in just short of Message Option 1, with 43/50 replies and a total success rate of 86%; not bad at all. Along with Message Option 1, this is also a complete custom-line, never seen before.

Additionally, the maths theme is also unheard of in this cosmos; the *Mona Lisa* of chat-up lines, if you will, which leaves you destined for success.

I will now analyse the responses to this line and address any curve-balls you may receive on the way.

Figure 6: Smooth

Today 14:36
Im trying to sort out my bills but I'm struggling with the math. What's 23-13?
10 darling x
What? No it's x
smoottthhhh x
GIF
Type a message ...

As seen in Figure 6, this line has gone to plan. The match answered with the number 10, knowing fully-well there's more to come. My confidant then comes in with the crusher line of 'What? No it's (name) x', and we get the golden-stamp response of 'smooth'.

However, don't be fooled. As seen below in Figure 7 you can't guarantee that your match will go along with the game-plan of this line but determination is key. If this happens and you feel disheartened, refer to the quote below.

''It's supposed to be hard. If it were easy, everyone would do it''.

Tom Hanks in A League of Their Own (presumably talking about Tinder).

Figure 7: The Curveball

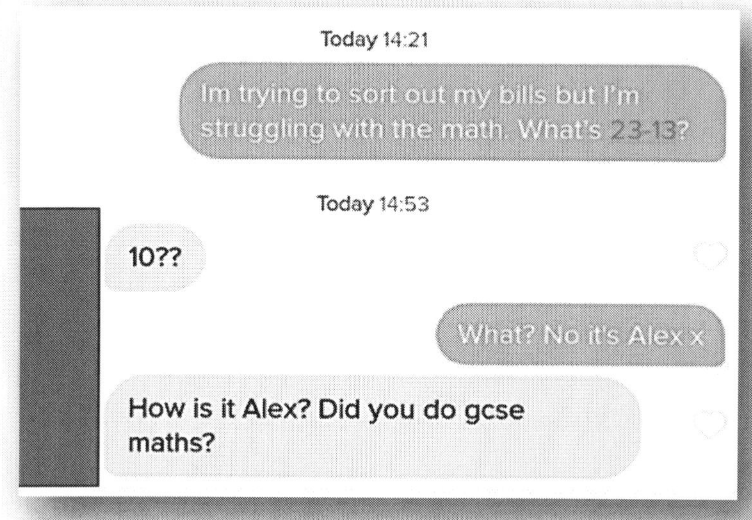

Today 14:21
Im trying to sort out my bills but I'm struggling with the math. What's 23-13?
Today 14:53
10??
What? No it's Alex x
How is it Alex? Did you do gcse maths?

Clearly, this match has struggled to understand the concept behind this line, but that's okay. I doubt in my confidant's wildest dreams he'd imagine receiving such an unearthly, rude and ignorant response to such a kind-hearted complement, especially when GCSE maths is compulsory in the UK. However, as seen below, my confidant did not give up, and boy did they reap the rewards.

Figure 8: From Rags to Riches

How is it Alex? Did you do gcse maths?
Because you're a 10/10 Alex
Best pick up line I have seen

This example speaks volumes. If my confidant did not persist with his efforts and let himself feel discouraged, this could have gone another way. However, his tenacity has served him well and, and according to Alex, this is the 'best pick up line' she has ever seen.

Such situations are echoed by the great words of Nelson Mandela (genuine quote): 'it always seems impossible until it is done'. For the more visual learners amongst us, see below.

<u>Figure 9 (Shutterstock.com)</u>

Continuing the line and chirpsing Alex.

Letting Alex discourage you.

Figure 10

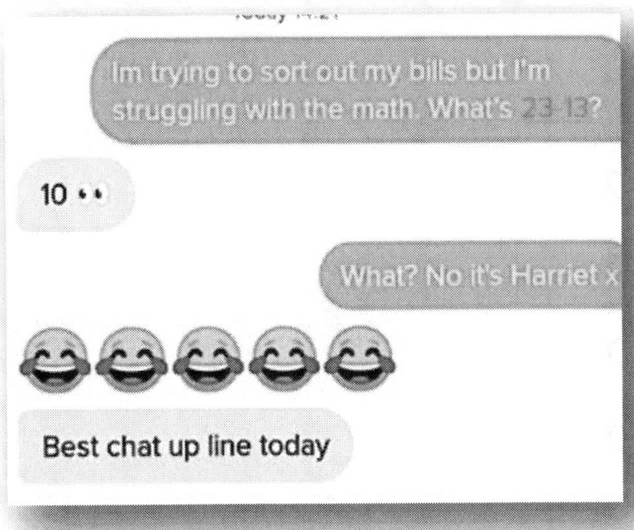

Im trying to sort out my bills but I'm struggling with the math. What's 23-13?
10
What? No it's Harriet x
Best chat up line today

The content of the response in Figure 10 is ideal. Two points are worth noting. Firstly, when your match sends the 'eyes emoji', this is a positive sign. This 'eyes emoji' is most commonly found in the 'you up *eyes*?' text that you may receive from a current-chirps.

Secondly, it is important not to be disheartened when your match doesn't respond with an 'x', either to your first message or even throughout conversations. Some people, most noticeably females, simply don't use the 'x' and view it as futile, but this is no reflection on how 'into' the conversation they really are. The lack of an 'x' may make the messages harder to 'read' in the sense of picking up signs of attraction, but fear not. This is just one more 'spanner in the works' in the obscure world that is Tinder, and you're no better placed to deal with such a spanner than after reading this guide.

<u>Figure 11: The nonexistence of the 'x' in Europe and the US</u>

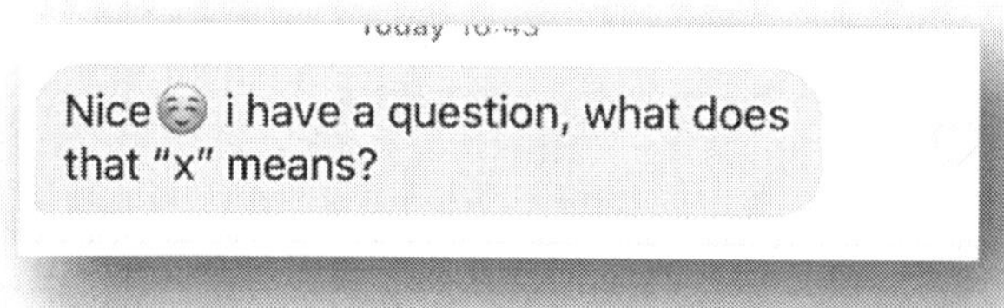

Nice i have a question, what does that "x" means?

When you look at Figure 11, you're no doubt left feeling slightly confused. Who on earth doesn't know what an 'x' means?

After lengthy periods of in-depth research, it appears that in multiple countries in Europe, as well as the US as a whole, the use of an 'x' is unprecedented, and therefore it's purpose will scarcely be understood. The match in Figure 10 is from Denmark and I've also gained a first-hand insight that the 'x' is also unheard of in the land of the Swedes.

You only need to briefly delve into the American forum website, Quora.com and you'll stumble across a multitude of questions such as:

1) 'Why do British people use an 'x' after every sentence in order to express something?

2) Why do people type 'x' at the end of their messages or comments? What does it mean?

3) When a British man uses 'xxx' in a text, how should I interpret it?

It is clear that the 'x', or use of, is simply one more thing to add to the list of excellent British ideas which Americans have failed to adopt, such as not allowing people to purchase a heavy-duty assault weapon as part of their weekly grocery-shop.

Figure 12: Academia

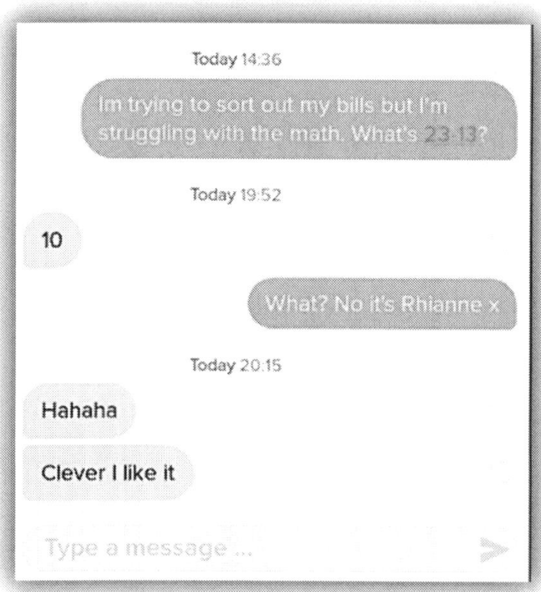

Today 14:36
Im trying to sort out my bills but I'm struggling with the math. What's 23-13?
Today 19:52
10
What? No it's Rhianne x
Today 20:15
Hahaha
Clever I like it
Type a message ...

For some, intelligence is an essential attribute of a match-worth-pursuing. If this applies to you then this is the line you've been waiting for. This line, with its academic theme and requirement of some mental, albeit simple, arithmetic, is the ideal way to suss out that ever-sought-after attribute.

Additionally, if intelligence in a match is what you're looking for, this is a hassle-free way of finding out before you waste any time 'chirpsing'.

Figure 13: Finding out you've wasted valuable chirps time

This is the last thing you want, as after all, time is money (see below).

'Time is more valuable than money, you can get more money, but you cannot get more time.' (Jim Rohn).

Well said, Jim.

First Message Option 3

You: 'Are you a bank loan? Because you've got my interest x'

This particular line received a mixed response in comparison to First Message Option 1 and 2 but that was to be expected. After all, the first two options really are gold dust and are tough to beat on the figures-front.

The 'bank loan line' received 39/50 replies which is still a high success rate of 78%. Now it must be said; this line is not an original of ours and we did find it on the internet. I always tread with caution when using such lines as it is highly possible that your match has heard it before and is therefore unlikely to reply. However, after extensive research my confidants and I have agreed that a 78% success rate is enough to warrant the line being chosen in our top 4 lines for this *comprehensive guide*.

Figure 14: The Financier

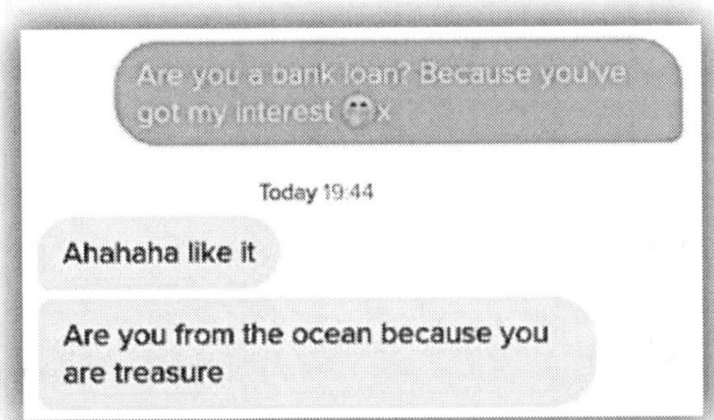

Are you a bank loan? Because you've got my interest 😛x
Today 19:44
Ahahaha like it
Are you from the ocean because you are treasure

You will scarcely be lucky enough to send out such a high-calibre line that you end up receiving a chat-up line in return. However, these rare moments are what you'll cherish most when you and your match have settled down and you leave this world behind.

This is a perfect response; approval of your line is granted and followed up by the compliment of literally comparing you to treasure off of the ocean floor; not bad for a day's work.

Figure 15: Smooth

Saturday 17:45
Are you a bank loan? Because you've got my interest x
Today 13:42
Ahh very smooth x

It's simple but effective. I'd always take 'smooth' as the golden stamp of approval that your line has had the desired-effect.

Figure 16: 10/10

Saturday 17:45
Are you a bank loan? Because you've got my interest x
Today 10:53
hahahaha
not heard that one before
10/10
wish i had enough money in my account to be a bank loan lmao

Figure 16 exhibits one of the more fascinating response we received from this line. It's interesting as this particular match states that they had never heard of this line which is always a positive sign.

As you delve further into the Tinder world, you'll find that lines which haven't been heard before are always more likely to generate a response. Such a point is well supported by the success rates of the completely original first lines in Options 1 and 2.

Additionally, this match appears to be lacking a basic understanding of private finance, but this can absolutely be overlooked when you're given a 10/10 rating for your first line.

First Message Option 4

You: 'Is there not a separate dating app for models?'

This line's multitude of unique aspects lands itself in the top 4 rankings of our *comprehensive guide*.

Firstly, it is unique in the literal sense. This is a complete custom of my confidants and I and we're incredibly proud to be able to share such a creation with our loyal followers.

Secondly, the use of a rhetorical question in a first line is usually unheard of but we've managed to make it happen.

Thirdly, this line probably comprises of the highest level of flattery seen amongst our first-lines, and such adulation is bound to land yourself a reply from your match, the future 'one'.

Despite the favourable aspects of this line, it did come in 4th place when it came down to the line-testing during the research phase. The 'model line' received 37/50 responses, with an overall success rate of 74%: a more than adequate outcome.

Figure 17: Humility

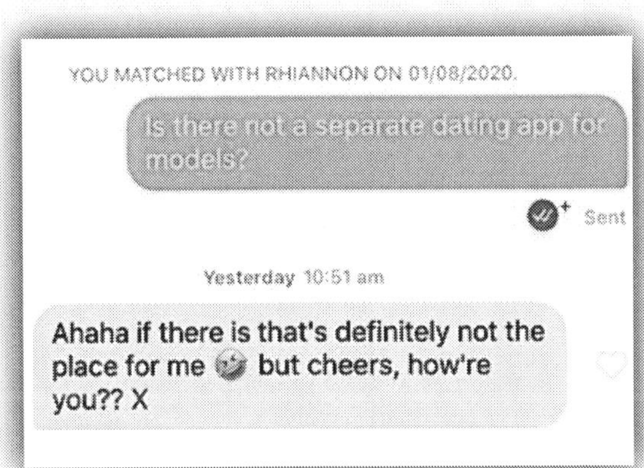

YOU MATCHED WITH RHIANNON ON 01/08/2020.
Is there not a separate dating app for models?
Sent
Yesterday 10:51 am
Ahaha if there is that's definitely not the place for me but cheers, how're you?? X

Wow. An ideal response for multiple reasons. Firstly, this match is displaying the utmost humility when being compared to a model; a positive sign from the outset. Secondly, this match is thankful for the compliment, and finally, has taken it upon themself to delve into the next phase; 'maintaining the chirps' (see Chapter 4).

Figure 18: Celebrate the small wins

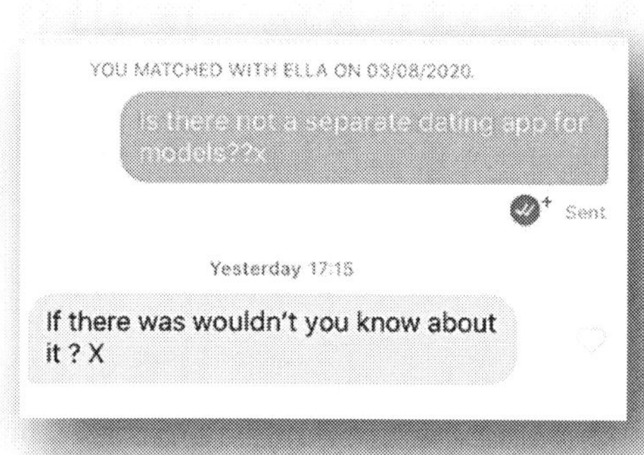

YOU MATCHED WITH ELLA ON 03/08/2020.
Is there not a separate dating app for models??x
Sent
Yesterday 17:15
If there was wouldn't you know about it ? X

Ah, the small wins. This is bound to put a spring in the step of any Tinder-user, and for good reason too. There seems to be a reoccurring theme here: the 'model line' seems to frequently generate a compliment in response to the line. This just goes to show, as with all things in life (except gambling), the more you put in, the more you get out.

Figure 19: Smooth: the 5* review

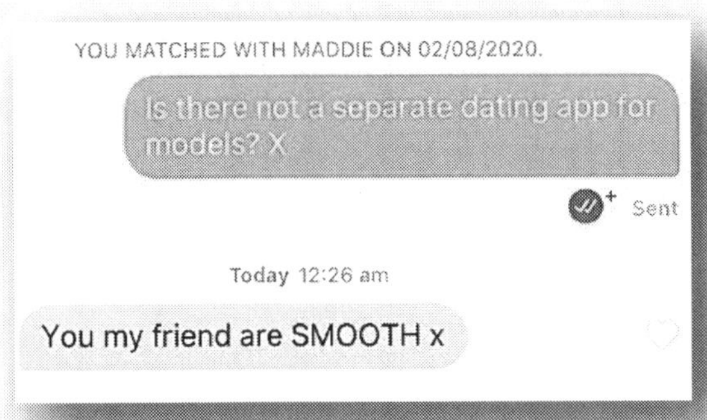
YOU MATCHED WITH MADDIE ON 02/08/2020.
Is there not a separate dating app for models? X
Sent
Today 12:26 am
You my friend are SMOOTH x

I think we can all agree that I have absolutely thrashed out the recognition of imminent success when you receive that ever-hallowed 'smooth' response.

Supplementary First Lines

As you can imagine, with any research-intensive project, you have material left over. Normally, this would end up in a miscellaneous file somewhere. Not on my watch.

My confidants and I discovered the few lines below that, while not always being as successful as the top 4, still generated effective responses. Due to the extensive work produced in relation to the top 4 lines, I feel that it is only necessary to outline one example per line below.

Figure 20: Walkabouts

YOU MATCHED WITH ESME ON 25/07/2020.
Sat 25 Jul, 16:47
Sorry my dog likes to go on walk abouts sometimes. Anyway now I'm in your dm's, how are you?x
Sent
Sat 25 Jul, 17:19
That was class
I'm good thanks how are you x

Warning: be mindful, be prudent, be cautious. This line can go one of two ways.

Firstly, the line can go as planned in Figure 20. Additionally, this line also has the effect of making you seem like an animal lover; who doesn't love a puppy?

The other way is a complete disaster. The issue which can arise is appearing like you are calling your match a dog. For obvious reasons, unless you are taking the 'treat them mean keep them keen theory' to an absolute extreme (advised against), this will likely have the opposite effect to the one desired unless when sending the line.

Figure 21: Today's date

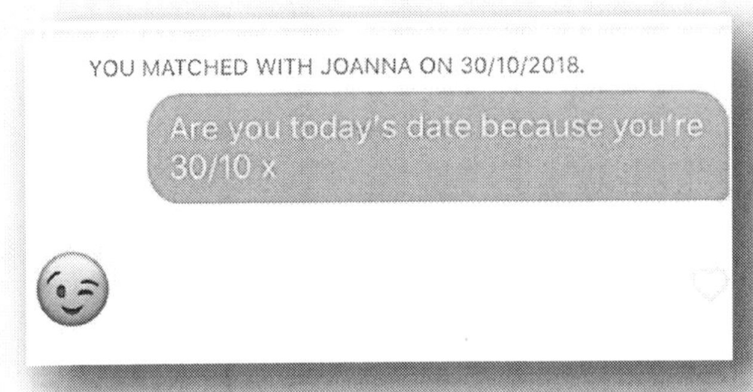

YOU MATCHED WITH JOANNA ON 30/10/2018.
Are you today's date because you're 30/10 x

When you refer to someone as a '10', you're suggesting that if you were to give them a 'rating' out of 10 on their looks, they would receive 10. For obvious reasons, this is highly complementary and is bound to impress your match. However, when this line is used effectively, this opens up a world of possibility to suggest that your match may have an obscene score, well above the 100% rating of 10/10.

This gives you the opportunity to exercise the utmost flattery while dishing out compliments like 49/11; mathematically questionable but romantically supreme.

The only drawback of this line is that its success will largely depend on, amongst other factors, the date. As you can imagine, if you were to refer to your match, or anybody in fact, as a 3/10 (3rd of October) they may be left feeling a little underwhelmed.

Figure 22: Keep it topical

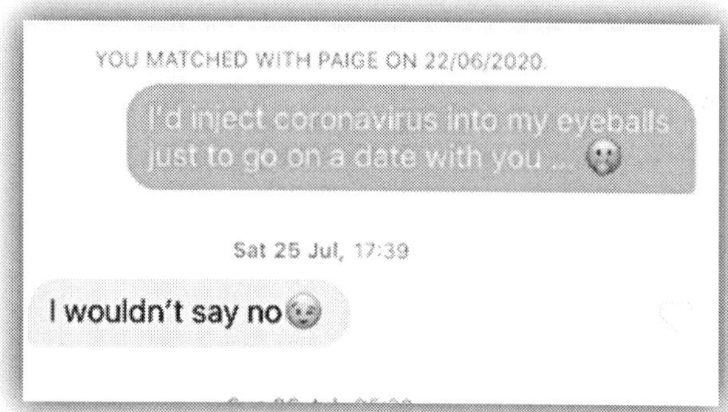

YOU MATCHED WITH PAIGE ON 22/06/2020.
I'd inject coronavirus into my eyeballs just to go on a date with you ...
Sat 25 Jul, 17:39
I wouldn't say no

Who doesn't love a topical first line? This match for one. Admittedly, this may only be valid for a few more months but its topical facet is bound to produce success for this period.

Lines to avoid

Here we have the bloopers. Whether the line lacks that attention-grabbing fizz, is simply too far or is on the tragic side of cheesy, we've highlighted those dreaded first lines to stay clear of.

Figure 23: The Athlete

I think this line's biggest pitfall is that it doesn't provide much room to generate a response. Or, the match may not be into sports. I guess we'll never know.

Figure 25: The Cretin

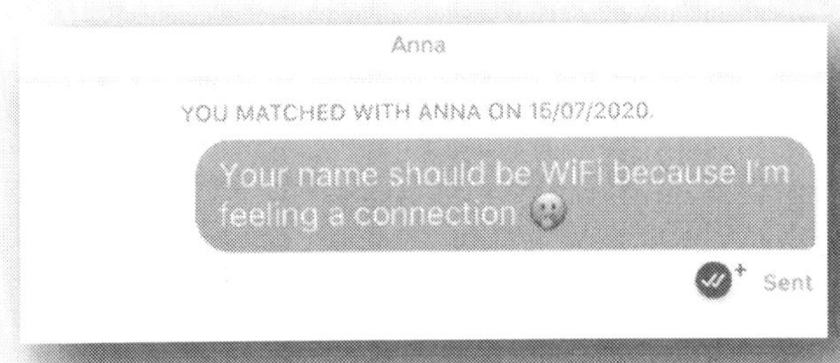

Anna
YOU MATCHED WITH ANNA ON 15/07/2020.
Your name should be WiFi because I'm feeling a connection
Sent

If this futile first line is to serve any purpose at all, it teaches us a lesson about the inadequacy of first lines taking from the internet. They are often far too cheesy and you'd have more luck pushing water uphill with a rake than receive a reply while using them.

Chapter 4: Moving from Tinder to another social media platform

While this could be explained in Chapter 4 (Maintaining the chirps), I think it is useful to emphasise the importance of moving to another platform beforehand. In the experience of my confidants and I, your chances of success in achieving the holy-grail (a Tinder date) are sufficiently enhanced when you move from Tinder to another platform. We have tried to undertake research on why this is, but we have had no success. We are unsure why success is enhanced after such a move, but it's just the way it is. I will now explain how to go about calculating this move and putting it into words, followed by reasons for making the move.

Let me set the scene: it's 6pm, the sun is setting, you lean over and pour yourself a large glass of Châteauneuf-du-Pape. You take a deep breath and reach for your phone in anticipation of replying to your match. The conversations been flowing and you're feeling confident.

Stop right there. It's time to make the move.

Do not reply to your match's last message until at least five hours has passed. This gives your next message authenticity. While you don't need to send this exact message, I would advise sending something along the lines of:

'As you can tell, my replies on here are really slow, could we speak on *Whatsapp or Snapchat' instead?*

For further guidance, refer to the examples below.

Figure 26

Also as you can probs tell my replies are woeful on here
Can we talk on something else like sc / WhatsApp??x
Wed 1 Jul, 11:47
Message me on WhatsApp, let's change it up from the usual boring snapchat conversations
x

Figure 27

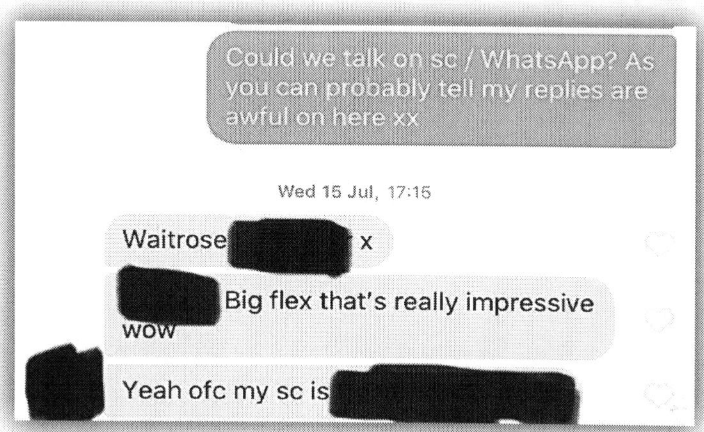

Could we talk on sc / WhatsApp? As you can probably tell my replies are awful on here xx
Wed 15 Jul, 17:15
Waitrose x
Big flex that's really impressive wow
Yeah ofc my sc is

Figure 28

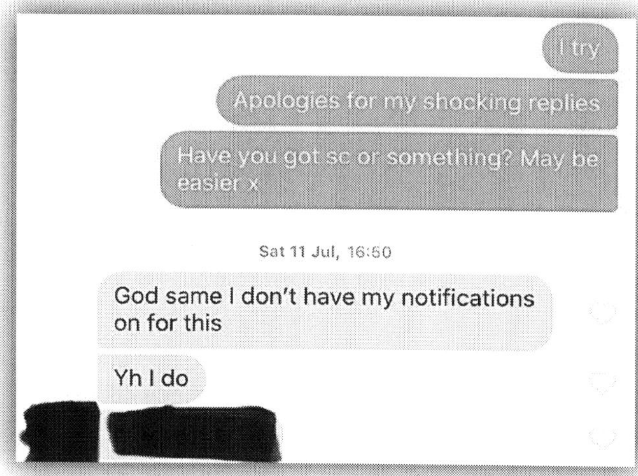

You will also need to decide which platform to choose for the question. After discussion with my confidants, we have decided that some indication on the best choice can be gained from reviewing the content of your match's messages and a lot can be gained from guessing correctly.

To use an illustration, you plan to buy your partner some flowers. Would they prefer you to ask what their favourite flowers are, or you guess correctly without asking? The same applies here.

<u>Whatsapp</u>

The typical Whatsapp-user can usually be sussed out from the formality of their messages. If they are using correct grammar throughout messages and usually sending full messages and fully-written words, you can be sure they're a Whatsapp user. Such signs could be the use of 'you' instead of 'u' or 'what are you up to?' instead of 'wuu2?'.

Snapchat

Character traits of a Snapchatter may include having more selfies on their Tinder profile, being more flirtatious over messages and just generally being more informal. They will often use text language and terms such as 'u', 'wuu2' as discussed above.

Social media platforms to avoid

It is imperative that you avoid Facebook at all costs. You are supposed to use Facebook to catch up with your middle-aged Aunt Linda; not to chirps the woman (or man) of your dreams.

If your match suggests talking on Kik or Plenty of Fish I would suggest blocking them on Tinder and potentially reporting them via the police non-emergency (101 for the UK).

Why is moving from Tinder to another platform a good idea?

Firstly, the general consensus is that people take a lot longer to reply on Tinder. While this is good in some cases as it stops conversations dying out, as you will see in the 'Maintaining the chirps' chapter, there will come a time where you need to move to another platform.

Additionally, some people are actually embarrassed to be using the platform itself, so they may often have their notifications turned off but this is unlikely to be the case for their other platforms such as Whatsapp or Snapchat.

Secondly, moving to another platform is the perfect opportunity to show your match that you are actually interested in them and you're not just going to waste their time. Additionally, in asking to move to another platform you can gain an insight into whether your match is actually interested in you at all or is simply entertaining your woeful small-talk. If your match gives you their number or Snapchat, you can take this as a green light to pursue with the next stages of ‘maintaining the chirps’ and eventually asking to go on a date.

Chapter 5: Maintaining the Chirps (Keeping the Conversation Going)

You're settling in nicely. You've popped that idyllic first line and it's gone down a treat. Now comes the hard part. That sought-after Tinder date will only come after enduring that strenuous chirpsing stage which will require you to effectively 'maintain the chirps' until the time comes for you to pop that petrifying first-date question. This is an incredibly stressful part of the process but thankfully my confidants and I will be here with you every step of the way.

I will run through my top tips for this stage as well as any morally offensive acts to avoid to ensure you don't fall at one of the last hurdles on this gruelling journey.

Firstly, you need to ensure that every message you send is thought-through to the finest detail. If you send your match a message that isn't leading, doesn't allow for an easy reply and consequently may end the conversation there and then, you're risking it all.

Every message has to be absolutely calculated: if you send a message that isn't leading and could potentially end the conversation, you are risking it all. As with anything in life, rushing is never going to end well. You can't rush the process. Good things take time.

For obvious reasons, I can't sit here and reel off every possible line to be using. In ensuring that you aren't rushing any replies, you can be certain that your replies will be full of good content and that you avoid any shooting yourself in the foot situations. The key advice to take from this is just to make sure that all messages can be replied to and are going to spark a response.

The quote below from nurturingmarriage.org summarises my point well.

'If you want something to last forever, you treat it differently' (F Burton Howard).

Frequency of messages

Here we have another critical issue, and one that, if not dealt with effectively, could trip you when you least expect it. There are no hard and fast rules but I will provide a rough framework based on the research we have conducted.

Figure 29

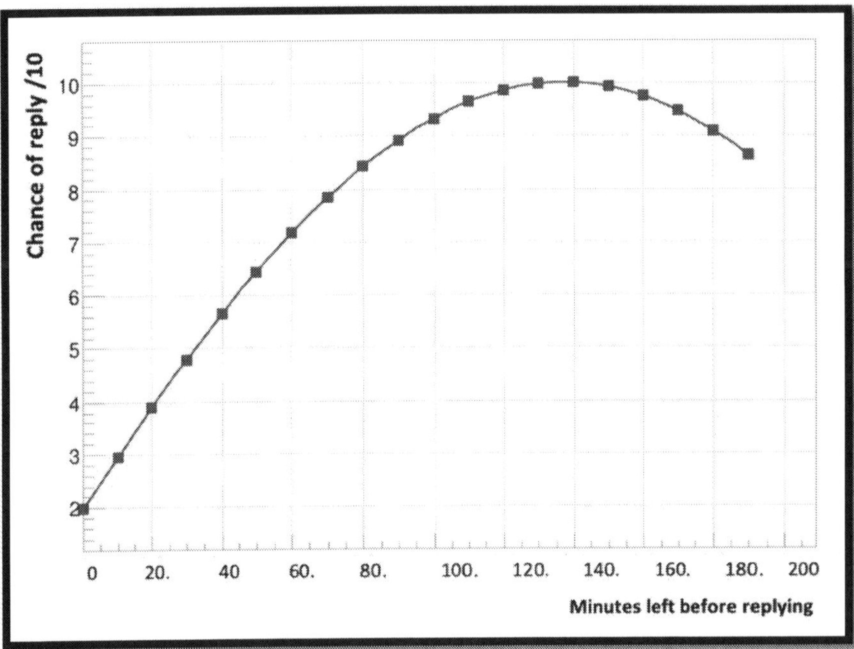

Thanks to my confidants and I putting in some serious legwork, we have managed compile a graph outlining the trends between how long you leave a Tinder message before replying, and your chance of receiving a reply as a result.

Of course, your chance of reply will not completely boil down to how long you leave the message for before replying. There is a multitude of factors which will affect this but we considered frequency of messages and how quickly you reply, to be of paramount importance in comparison to other factors.

As can be seen from the graph in Figure 29, the optimum amount of time you should leave before replying is somewhere between the 120 -140-minute mark (2 hours - 2 hours and 20 minutes). To take an example, if you woke up and 8am and went to bed at 11pm, this would allow you to exchange roughly 8 sets of messages, but this will depend on how quickly your match replies to your message. This allows for the conversation to remain interesting and avoids a situation where you run out of things to say which is the ultimate hindrance between you and that sought-after Tinder date.

There will come a time during every Tinder escapade, where you will need to find out where your match lives. Let me be clear, I'm not talking postcodes; just a rough idea so you can assess whether it's too far away.

Unless you have your Tinder distance set to the exact kilometre distance you'd be willing to travel (which is rarely the case; usually the distance is set further for most Tinder users) then you will need to pose this question at some point. This is also a good method of building rapport with your match and is also a fairly typical stock-line in you'll find in any good chirpsing-manual. This is important to find out relatively early so you're not wasting your own or your match's time. However, extreme caution must be taken. This question, depending on how you ask it, could be viewed by your match as quite strange.

I would advise using something similar to the line in Figure 30 below, and waiting at least 24 hours after you begin talking before asking this question. This is also essential, as asking it as one of your first messages will likely look too keen and put off your match.

Remember the hallowed theory: 'Treat them mean, keep them keen' (Martin Luther King, Jr. 1935).

Figure 30

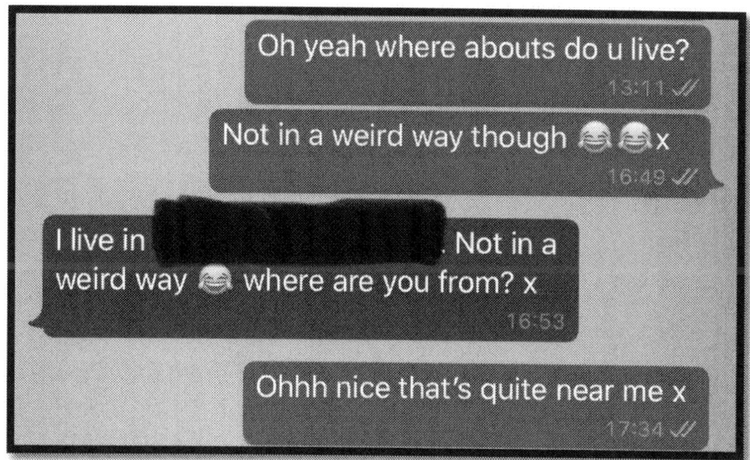

Oh yeah where abouts do u live?
13:11
Not in a weird way though 😂😂x
16:49
I live in . Not in a weird way 😂 where are you from? x
16:53
Ohhh nice that's quite near me x
17:34

Here my confidant has followed strict protocol and moved to another platform (Whatsapp in this case) quite soon into the conversation.

Additionally, whether you use a laughing emoji after the line is up to you. However, if you do I would always advise sending two instead of one and the use of an ‘x’ to soften the potentially harsh tones of the message.

<u>Follow up lines which can be used in general conversation</u>

i) How was your day?

I know what you’re thinking. Hang on, this is child’s play. Yes, it is, but some people need to be guided every step of the way and that’s what we’re here for. The fairy godmothers of Tinder, if you will. This is a classic line and can shortly be followed by the line below.

ii) Whatcha get up to today?

This line is often undervalued. It’s very effective as it usually produces something else to talk about and consequently keeps the conversation alive. Please see the example below.

You: whatcha get up to today?
Match: Nothing much really just had work, what about you?

And then you can ask what they do for work; genius, I know.

Conversation-preservation is the key. Keeping the conversation alive is ultimately the most important aspect of this process. This is because after a few days of this conversation-preservation, you'll get to the stage of popping that momentous question regarding the holy grail; the *Tinder date*.

Additionally, pay close attention to the use of 'whatcha' instead of 'what did you'. It's hard to describe what effect this has but it certainly spices things up which can help you avoids any mundane vibes.

iii) Something along the lines of 'What do you do?' i.e. studying or working

This line is also bound to produce further conversation; the key ingredient to any successful Tinder-romance.

Follow up line to the previous question; a classic

iv) **I mean presumably you're model but just wondering if you do anything else on the side?**

If there's anything I've learnt from this research project, it's that people enjoy being called models. Period.

This line also entails the key aspects of humour, wit and flattery.

What do I do if my match ignores a message of mine?

v) **Just a heads up I think your phone may be broken because it says you've opened my message but I haven't received a reply...**

Now let me make clear that this is not a bullet-proof message and success cannot be guaranteed, as they may be ignoring you because they simply don’t want to pursue anything.

However, if the match is still viable, this message is the life-line you so desperately need.

Chapter 6: Popping the question (Asking your match to go on a date)

If you've got to this stage you can count your lucky stars that you're through the worst of it. If you're in a position where you feel confident enough to pop the question then give yourself a pat on the back. All that hard work and dedication to the cause has paid off. However, just because you may feel like your match may agree to a date, does not mean they necessarily will.

The success, or lack of such a question will largely boil down to three components:

1) How long you talk (chirps) your match for before proposing the date
2) How you word the actual question
3) What day you arrange the date for. In other words, how many days pass between asking the question and actually attending the date.

I will now elaborate on these key issues.

How long should I talk to my match for before asking to go on a date?

As with anything in this Tinder process, there is no hard and fast rule for how long you should talk for, but we can offer some guidelines to work from.

We would advise asking the question between 3-5 days after the first day you began talking. So, for example, if you begin talking on Monday evening you should be safe (providing the conversation is flowing) to ask to go on a date any day from Thursday onwards.

If you ask the question before the 3-day period, you run the risk of coming across as too eager and your match will likely feel like they don't know you well enough yet. Hold tight.

If you leave it too long before asking the question the conversation will likely have started to die down and you may well have run out of chat which would no doubt be an absolute calamity.

How should I word the question?

This part is fairly hassle free and you have two options. You can either go for the 'date' option or 'doing something' option. Please refer to the examples below to get a better idea.

Option 1: Doing something-simple

'Do you fancy doing something this week? Could be fun x'

Option 2: Date-simple

'Do you fancy going on a date sometime? Could be fun x'

Option 3: Uber-confident

You: 'Have you got many plans this week?'
Match (hopefully): 'No nothing much what about you?'
You: 'Oh perfect plenty of time for our date then'

What day should I arrange the date for? (How long after asking)

This part of the process is arguably the most delicate and consequently, must be handled with the utmost care.

The amount of times I have seen fellow users organise a date and further down the line, fall victim to their match's cold feet, is genuinely frightful.

Cold feet defined (urbandictionary.com)

To get cold feet means to lose your desire or nerve to do something. Often people 'get cold feet' because they get nervous.

For example, sometimes the bride or groom might not show up to their wedding (or Tinder date) because they've gotten cold feet.

While the research on this particular issue is scarce, and arguably no cure will be found, certain steps can be taken to reduce the risk of falling victim to the harshest of surprises; the cancelled Tinder date.

As you can probably tell, this takes meticulous planning. Firstly, if you know you are not free to meet up with your match in the next few days (I would recommend four maximum) then simply wait until you are before popping that golden question.

The main reason for this is that maintaining the chirps, despite reading that particular iconic chapter of this book, becomes incredibly hard after the first few days. There is only so much content you can provide to your match before the conversation starts to dry up. If you maintain a golden-chirps for three days, pop the question and then have to attempt to chirps for another five days (for example) you really are fighting a losing battle. By ensuring that you organise the date within three days after your match agrees to said date, you put yourself in the best possible position to i) avoid cold-feet and ii) avoid all your hard work crumbling in front of you in the form of a dying-chirps.

If you still can't see the potential hazards of organising a date for more than three days in advance, please refer to Figure 31.

Figure 31: Don't do it

Chapter 7: Recovering a Dying Chirps (Saving a conversation which is going badly, or has finished)

What's a dying-chirps you ask? A dying (or dead) chirps can be broadly described as the situation where you were once talking to someone on Tinder when all was well, but the conversation has since deteriorated (or is on its way there) to the point of the chat-content being dull (dying), or you have stopped talking altogether (dead).

The dying, or even worse, dead chirps is the stuff of nightmares. No one likes to have hard work go down the drain but to see 'the one' slowly slip through the sand in front of your very eyes; no one deserves that.

But fear not. There are some simple techniques which can be used to revive that dead chirps; the defibrillators of the Tinder world.

The Dying Chirps

If the conversation is dying i.e. the conversation is becoming dull

If you believe you are falling victim to a dying-chirps, I would suggest majorly ramping up the rate of conversation with the highest quality of chat. Ideally you would do this all within one day so that by the time it comes to popping the question, the chirpsometer is flying off the radar.

Once you exchange these four or five good quality messages then pop the question along the lines of:

'I know it's hard to believe but my chat is even better in person. Shall we just go on a date??'

This highlights the quality of the conversation and alludes to it being even better in the future; a difficult prospect for any match to turn down.

The Last-Ditch Effort

If the conversation is dead i.e. you have been ignored

Two possible causes are worth exploring.

Firstly, there is a perfectly good explanation for why your match hasn't replied. Possibly they were busy at the time of seeing your message or they were thinking of a reply and got distracted.

Secondly, they ignored you because they think you're a worthless cretin and have no interest in you whatsoever. You'd have more luck convincing Nigel Farage to attend an Extinction Rebellion protest[1] than receive a reply from this particular match.

There is no magic formula for finding out which cause is to blame. However, whether you receive a reply to the line below or not should push you in the right direction.

---

[1] (Google: Youtube Nigel Farage Vs Extinction Rebellion Protestor

The Line

You: Sorry to hear about your phone

Match: What?

You: Oh, I thought it was broken as I messaged you but I can't see a reply'

It is essential that if you do receive a reply to this line (which will likely be laughter of sorts), your next message must also be interesting and generate a response otherwise you risk finishing off the conversation for good.

Chapter 8: Is Tinder Plus or Tinder Gold worth it?

In a nutshell, yes.

When you hear the words 'Tinder Plus' or 'Tinder Gold' the word tragic probably springs to mind. For me, I hear *margins*. The returns you get in terms of increased matches, albeit not financial, are more than worth it. In return for that small monthly investment ranging between £1.92 and £7.49 per month depending on how many months you pay for in one go, these puppies can turn your Tinder life upside down; and not in a bad way.

In comparison to the free Tinder, these two paid versions simply blow it out of the water. If they were cars, the free version of Tinder would be a beaten-up old Ford KA while Tinder Plus and Gold would be more of a supercar type. They are simply incomparable.

Figure 33: Tinder: Free Version (Usedandwell.co.uk)

I will now explain each additional feature you get when you pay for either Plus or Gold followed by an analysis of each perk and a breakdown of the pricing structure.

Tinder Plus

Unlimited Swipes

The lack of a limit on your swipes per day is arguably the greatest perk that comes with Tinder Plus. There is nothing worse than spending a whole evening swiping while searching for 'the one' to be smacked in the face with that dreaded notification; 'You're Out of Likes'.

Figure 34: We Hate To See It

I believe an analogy is the most effective way to really emphasise the benefits of this feature. Imagine that you are at a fairground playing that game where you throw a hoop over a bottle and you win a cuddly toy. Your potential matches are cuddly toys and you only have 5 hoops to throw. Tinder Plus gives you unlimited hoops. Let it be clear; opportunities like this don't come about often.

Location Change: Tinder Plus allows you to fake your location

I struggle to see the attraction of this feature but I suppose it could come in handy for some. Perhaps you are looking for a Thai-bride of sorts. 'Whatever ruffles your truffles' springs to mind. Moving on.

Super Likes

The 'super like' increases your chance of being viewed by your potential match three-fold.

Roses delivered to the door? How about a box of classy chocolates? A horse and carriage? Shove a super like in your pipe and smoke it; the beacon of romance.

Anyone with the measliest amount of Tinder experience knows fully well that a super like can only be compared to such gestures above.

The every-day Tinder user, the freeloader, if you will, receives just 1 super like per day.

This ultimately puts you in a predicament when you come across someone who you may think is worthy of this beacon of romance. Is it worth it? Is the grass greener on the other side? You just don't know, no one knows.

All of this uncertainty ceases to exist when you have 5 super likes while subscribed to Tinder Plus or Gold. It is the ideal amount. If you're in a position where you feel like you need more than 5 super likes per day I think the platform may be taking a hold of you.

Remember, when the fun stops, stop (Sennet Group 2015 (Gambling industry-funded responsible betting body)).

Boosts

The boost. Do not get me started on the boost.

Tinder Plus and Tinder Gold come with one free boost per month. This increases your profiles viewings 10-fold for 30 minutes. The results really do speak for themselves. Additionally, while using the free version of Tinder you would have to fork out £6.99 for one single boost which makes that £1.92 investment per month seem like a drop in the ocean.

Throughout the mass of research conducted by my confidants and I, we have never experienced a boost which achieved less than twenty matches. 'Twenty matches???' I hear you mutter under your breath in absolute disbelief. Yes, t w e n t y.

You could spend weeks aimlessly swiping with your right thumb on the absolute brink of collapse and you wouldn't receive such a result.

You may be sat there with a few sterling in the bank thinking, what next? Should I short Tesla stock after one more of Elon Musk's ever-more common stock-crippling stunts? Should I ride with Ocada for the long run? No. If I could give you one investment tip, I'd say invest in yourself. Invest in Tinder Plus.

Undo last swipe

It's another lonely Saturday night and you're swiping right on your Tinder faster than the spread of COVID-19 in Boohoo's Leicester factory. You make the mistakes of all mistakes. You forget to 'super like' the one.

Now, at this point if you were a free Tinder you'd be so utterly ashamed of yourself for carrying out such a mindless error that you'd take yourself to bed with a warm cup of cocoa, and rightly so.

However, if you were paying for Plus or Gold you'd simply hit that rewind button with the satisfaction of knowing fully-well that you are reaping the rewards of your investments.

Tinder Gold

Who Likes Me"

Tinder Gold has an additional feature where you are told as soon as someone has swiped right on you. You can then either swipe right on them and begin the plummeting nosedive into their DMs or politely swipe left.

This avoids the painful situation where you have to keep swiping through until you find someone who has already liked you. This makes finding ‘the one’ seem a lot more like finding a needle in a haystack than any remotely enjoyable process. The Tinder waters are choppy as they are and this additional hindrance definitely does not provide for smooth sailing.

Top Picks

According to Tinder this feature ‘surfaces a curated list of your best potential matches’. However, I have scarcely matched with someone on here.

Here we have a dilemma. The benefits of the 'Who Likes You' feature in terms of saving valuable swiping time simply cannot be underplayed. However, this is the only beneficial feature of Tinder Gold. The 'Top Picks' feature is futile in my humble opinion and makes it difficult to justify spending nearly double the amount on the upgrade from Plus to Gold.

In summary, if you have enough time to swipe a lot on Tinder, I would advise only going for the Plus Option as you can still reap the rewards providing you put in the hard swiping-work. If you are strapped for time then maybe the additional investment in Gold is more up your street.

Ultimately as with any investment the pros and cons alongside what capital you're willing to risk need to be considered. Book a meeting with your FA and take the table below along to it.

Figure 35: Markets, Know Your Markets (www.datingscout.co.uk)

Duration / Credits / Coins	Costs	Total
	Tinder Plus	
1 Month	4.99 GBP / Month	4.99 GBP
6 Months	2.50 GBP / Month	15.00 GBP
12 Months	1.92 GBP / Month	23.04 GBP
	Tinder Gold	
1 Month	7.49 GBP / Month	7.49 GBP
3 Months	9.32 GBP / Month	27.96 GBP
12 Months	3.50 GBP / Month	42.00 GBP

Chapter 9: All good things must come to an end

It brings me great pain to say that this is the end of our journey together. There is no excuse for your Tinder chat to be anything other than poetry. You should be the Tinder equivalent of Daniel Craig in a pair of blue swimming trunks, emerging from the ocean in slow motion at a Caribbean beach resort. Undoubtedly, you'll be muttering lines about overheating laptops and bank interest rates in your sleep by now, so it's time to put the wheels into motion.

Needless to say, these skills are almost as transferable as the word "teamwork" on your resumé, and they apply across the multitude of other dating apps that are out there.

Who's to say that, because of this advice, you won't meet your Mr/Mrs Right. Who's to say you won't strike-up a Jane Austin-style romance. Who's to say that, ten or so years down the line, you won't be sat in traffic doing the school-run, with three crying children in the back of your MPV and a mortgage the size of the Greek budget deficit, wishing that you never bought this fucking book in the first place.

Printed in Great Britain
by Amazon